THE WORLD

ASTRONOMY

Carole Stott

KINGFISHER

KINGFISHER

Kingfisher Publications Plc
New Penderel House,
283–288 High Holborn,
London WC1V 7HZ
www.kingfisherpub.com

First published by Kingfisher Publications Plc 2006
10 9 8 7 6 5 4 3 2 1

1TR/1105/TIMS/PICA(PICA)/128MA/F

Copyright © Kingfisher Publications Plc 2006

First published in 2003 as *The Best-Ever Book of Astronomy*

ISBN-13: 978 0 7534 1343 2
ISBN-10: 0 7534 1343 4

Editor: Catherine Brereton
Designer: Mark Bristow
Cover designer: Heidi Appleton
Consultant: Dr Margaret Penston, Institute of Astronomy,
University of Cambridge (for the Royal Astronomical Society)
Indexer: Sue Lightfoot
Senior production controllers: Nancy Roberts, Lindsey Scott
DTP manager: Sarah Pfitzner
Picture research: Rachael Swann
Artwork archivists: Wendy Allison, Jenny Lord

The website addresses listed in this book are correct at the time of
going to print. However, due to the ever-changing nature of the
internet, website addresses and content can change. Websites can
contain links that are unsuitable for children. The publisher cannot
be held responsible for changes in website addresses or content, or
for information obtained through third-party websites. We strongly
advise that internet searches should be supervised by an adult.

Printed in China

The Publisher would like to thank the **Royal
Astronomical Society** for their help and
co-operation in the production of this book.

Since its formation in 1820, the fellows of the
Royal Astronomical Society have worked to
advance astronomy and geophysics through
front-line scientific research. The Society gives
grants for scientific work, and distributes results
throughout the world – at meetings, by the written
word and on the web. The Society provides
information and advice to young people who are
thinking of becoming astronomers or geophysicists,
and to their teachers.

Further information about the Society can be
obtained from its website: **www.ras.org.uk**

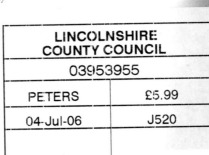

CONTENTS

LOOKING AT THE UNIVERSE — 4–5

Earth's eye view — 6–7

The earliest astronomers — 8–9

The centre of the Universe — 10–11

Looking closer — 12–13

Astronomer at work — 14–15

Tools of the trade — 16–17

Observatory Earth — 18–19

Invisible Universe — 20–21

Space explorers — 22–23

THE SOLAR SYSTEM	24–25	THE REALM OF THE STARS	46–47
The Sun	26–27	Seeing stars	48–49
Earth: home planet	28–29	Giants and dwarfs	50–51
Earth's Moon	30–31	Explosive finish	52–53
Rock worlds	32–33	Islands in the Universe	54–55
Near neighbours	34–35	Life	56–57
Spacerocks	36–37	Beginning to end	58–59
The King	38–39	REFERENCE	
Ringed worlds	40–41	Glossary	60–61
Planetary moons	42–43	Index	62–63
Ice kingdoms	44–45	Acknowledgements	64

LOOKING AT THE UNIVERSE

From Earth we can look out into the Universe. People have always done this. Many have simply enjoyed the splendour of a starry sky or gazed in wonder at the brilliant Moon. Others have done more than wonder, and have investigated what these places are like. The scientific study of the stars and planets is called astronomy, and the men and women who do this work are astronomers. They reveal the Universe's fascinating sights and intriguing worlds for everyone to understand and enjoy. They also explain how everything fits together, and how the Universe changes with time. They have even pieced together its past and predicted its future.

Studying the Universe

Unlike other scientists, who get close to what they study, astronomers have to work at long distance. They use a range of tools and techniques to study the stars and planets from Earth. Their most fundamental tool is the telescope. Yet, there is much to be seen by eye alone. Take your first step to becoming an astronomer by simply looking up and into the Universe.

What is the Universe?

The Universe is everything that exists. That is the Earth, everything on the Earth and everything that surrounds our planet. It includes the smallest particles and the largest galaxies, frozen planets, explosive stars, holes in space and life itself. Everything in the Universe is made of the same chemical elements that we find on Earth, and the laws of science that operate on Earth also govern the whole Universe.

Looking up

Professional astronomers use powerful telescopes housed in mountain-top observatories (left). Amateur astronomers use their eyes, binoculars or a portable telescope (right).

Galaxies

Astronomers are discovering new things all the time. At the start of the 20th century, we knew of only one galaxy. Now we know there are billions of them, including the Sombrero (top) and M33 (right).

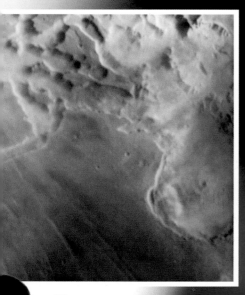

Planets

For over 40 years, astronomers have used spaceprobes to work in space on their behalf. These have shown views of the planets that are not possible from Earth, like this image of the surface of Mars (above).

The Moon

By studying Earth's relationship with the Moon, astronomers learned that gravity is universal. Everything in the Universe has gravity and is affected by it.

Earth

By investigating the Universe around us, we learn more about our home planet, Earth. We have learned about its past, present and future.

Earth's eye view

Look up from the Earth at a cloudless
sky and you look out into the Universe.
Whichever way you look there are stars.
In the daytime sky, just one is visible – its
light illuminates our sky and it outshines
all the other stars. It is the Sun. The Sun
is so close that it should never be looked at
directly. Its brilliant light can damage our
eyes. At night, we see a sky full of much
more distant stars. Each appears fixed on
a backdrop which moves with time. The
Moon and planets travel across the starry
background. Occasionally a passing
visitor, such as a comet, adds to the view.

Starry sky
Exactly what you see of the Universe depends
on where you look from, the direction you look
in, the date and the time. In all cases, the most
common object you'll see is a star. Each one is
a star in our Milky Way Galaxy. A bright milky
path across your sky means you are looking
towards the heart of the Galaxy.

Star patterns
The brightest stars
in the night sky make
up the constellation
patterns. Stars differ
not only in brightness
but also in colour, size
and distance. A red
supergiant marks a
shoulder of Orion, the
hunter, and the Orion
Nebula, a vast cloud
of gas and dust, is the
sword hanging from
his belt of stars.

Close-up view

The Moon is the closest space object to Earth and is easily seen in our sky. Using just our eyes we can make out features on its surface. With binoculars or a telescope we can see much more. Far larger and more distant objects, such as planets and galaxies, appear much smaller than the Moon but are easy enough to spot. Their details are revealed to us through telescopes based on Earth and in space.

The Moon and planets

Neither the Moon nor the planets have light of their own, but shine by reflected sunlight. They are always found within a particular strip of sky, which circles around Earth. This sky band is made of 12 constellations collectively called the zodiac. The Moon and planets travel across the backdrop of the zodiac, constellation after constellation. The band circles around us, roughly above Earth's equator. Wherever you are on Earth, you can look towards the zodiac band to see the Moon and planets.

The earliest astronomers

The first people to look up at the sky and wonder about what they saw were the earliest astronomers. These observers, watching the sky thousands of years ago, drew imaginary pictures around the stars, identified five planets, and used the movements of the Sun and Moon across the sky for keeping track of time. Whether in Europe, Africa or Asia, they created myths and stories about the sky and what is in it. There was much they did not know about the Universe, and what they did not understand they often feared.

Fear of the unknown
Ancient Chinese astronomers recorded many comets and eclipses. But the sudden appearance of a comet or the darkening of the Sun during an eclipse caused real fear. They believed a dragon was trying to eat the Sun. Drums and gongs were banged and arrows shot into the sky to scare the dragon away.

Egyptian Universe
The ancient Egyptians believed that their sky goddess, Nut, arched over the Earth. Her body was made of stars and appeared in our sky as the path of the Milky Way. Nut was held up by Shu, the god of light and air. Below them was Nut's husband Geb, the god of the Earth.

First observatories

Over the centuries, astronomers began to make sense of what they saw. They made regular observations, took measurements, listed the stars, and explained how parts of the known Universe fitted together. Buildings and monuments were built for astronomical use. The Mayan people built the Caracol Temple in Mexico (above left) around a thousand years ago. Its windows are positioned so that Venus can be seen through them on special dates.

Calendar

Many peoples developed calendars, based on the daily and yearly movement of the Sun in the sky and the changing shape of the Moon. The Aztecs, living in Central America around 500 years ago, had their own accurate calendar. Their Sun god is in the centre and the days are carved around him.

Spread of knowledge

People living in different parts of the world worked independently to find out about the Universe. The Babylonians, living in the Near East over 4,000 years ago, had the most advanced astronomical knowledge of ancient times. They knew little compared to today's astronomers, but our present knowledge can be traced back to their beginnings. The work of the Babylonians was built on by the ancient Greeks, and in turn was developed and passed to medieval Europe by Arabic-speaking peoples.

Measuring

In about 200BCE, the Greek astronomer Eratosthenes measured the size of Earth. He compared the way sunlight struck the ground at Syrene and at Alexandria in Egypt at the same time on midsummer's day. He then used his findings to work out the distance around Earth.

The centre of the Universe

Astronomers of the ancient world believed that the Earth was the centre of the Universe, and that the Sun and other objects travelled around it. These beliefs and other astronomical knowledge were collected together in a book called *Almagest*, by the Greek astronomer Claudius Ptolemy, who lived in the 2nd century. Ptolemy's view of the Universe was accepted until the 16th century, when a revolutionary idea changed astronomers' minds. Nicolaus Copernicus developed a new explanation of how the known Universe fitted together. He believed the Sun was at its centre. Later astronomers agreed and proved him right.

Revolutionary thinking
Copernicus' belief that Earth and the other planets move around the Sun was presented in his book *De Revolutionibus Orbium Coelestium* in 1543. Its publication marked a turning point in our understanding of the Universe.

Changing ideas

For thousands of years, astronomers thought the Universe contained much less than it really does. They knew of Earth, its Moon, and five other planets – Mercury, Venus, Mars, Jupiter and Saturn. They believed that Earth stood still, as the Sun, Moon and planets circled around it, and that a sphere of stars marked the edge of the Universe. This idea was replaced by Copernicus' system, which contained the same parts, but had the Sun fixed as everything circled around it. This matched what astronomers saw in the sky. The Danish astronomer Tycho Brahe spent 20 years making detailed observations, and the German astronomer Johannes Kepler used these observations to explain the paths (orbits) of the known planets around the Sun.

Earth-centred
Ptolemy's view of the Universe has the Earth at the centre. The Moon, Mercury, Venus, Sun, Mars, Jupiter and Saturn all travel around it. A sphere of stars circle it and, in this picture, God watches over it all.

Sun-centred
Copernicus's view has the Sun at the centre. Earth is the third planet from the Sun and travels around it every year. The Moon travels around Earth. A circle of stars marks the edge of the Universe and is represented by the 12 zodiac constellations.

Johannes Kepler
Kepler explained that planets orbit in ellipses, not circles. He showed that each planet moves fastest near the Sun and slower further away, and that more distant planets orbit at slower speeds.

The Universe today

Astronomers of the past believed they could see the whole Universe. In fact they saw only a tiny fraction of it – just the parts they could see with their eyes. Today, we know there is much more, and we know it is not centred on the Sun. The Sun is just one of the billions of stars that are the Milky Way Galaxy. The Milky Way is just one of billions of galaxies in the Universe. Wherever we look there are galaxies, and if we could look at the Universe from another galaxy, the view would be just the same.

Tycho Brahe
Tycho Brahe was an outstanding observer who accurately measured the positions of stars and planets. He developed and used special measuring instruments, such as his astronomical quadrant.

Looking closer

For centuries, people had thought they could see all of the Universe, and that our planet with its Moon was unique. In the early 17th century, astronomers started to use the newly invented telescope to look up at the sky. From 1609, the Italian Galileo Galilei studied the Moon, the planets and the stars. He detected four moons circling Jupiter, found that the Milky Way is packed full of stars, and that Venus has phases like the Moon. Over the next three centuries, astronomers discovered more of the Universe, learned what stars are made of, and started to piece together the story of the Universe and everything in it.

Starry Messenger
Galileo Galilei published his discoveries about the planets, moons and stars in a book called *Starry Messenger* (1610). It was a sensation and made him a celebrity. More importantly, his observations showed what momentous discoveries were possible using the telescope, and how such discoveries could change the course of astronomical history.

Collecting light

Early telescopes were refractors, which means they used lenses to collect light. Soon the reflector, which uses mirrors, was developed. From 1666, the English scientist Isaac Newton experimented with light and mirrors. He made a reflecting telescope and showed how a glass prism (right) can be used to split light into a spectrum – the rainbow band of seven colours. Today, instruments called spectroscopes allow astronomers to split starlight into spectra, and identify the chemical elements in a star.

First telescopes

The very first telescopes, such as the one Galileo used, were about as powerful as a pair of simple binoculars today. A lens at the sky-end of a tube collected light. This was directed down the tube to the eye-end where a smaller lens formed the light into an image of the object observed.

Biggest telescope

Herschel built increasingly powerful reflectors. His 12m-long telescope (below), in use from 1789, was the biggest and most powerful telescope of its day. It had a mirror that was 1.2m in diameter.

Tracking the stars

Astronomers in the 18th century concentrated on measuring the positions of objects in the sky. Much of the cataloguing and mapping was done at national observatories. Amateur astronomers also played their part. William Herschel took up astronomy as a hobby but became one of the most famous astronomers of all time. He was an excellent observer and an outstanding instrument-maker. He would systematically sweep his telescopes across the sky, helped by his sister Caroline who recorded many of his observations. Herschel discovered the planet Uranus in 1781. He also discovered around 2,500 star clusters, nebulae and galaxies.

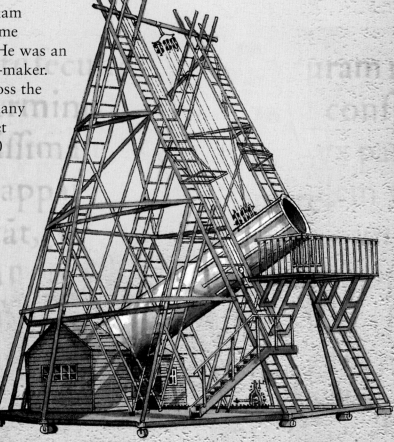

Moon watching

Galileo saw mountains on the Moon, and what he thought were seas. Today, we know the Moon is dry, but we still use Galileo's name *mare* (Latin for 'sea') for the large smooth basins on the Moon's surface. These two drawings appeared in his book *Starry Messenger*.

Astronomer at work

Astronomers have been looking up at the sky and trying to make sense of the Universe for thousands of years. Over the centuries, they have made astonishing discoveries and answered many questions, but there is always more to investigate. Most of the 8,000 or so professional astronomers studying the Universe today work in universities worldwide. Others work in government-run organizations and space agencies. They collect information from space, and spend their time processing and interpreting it. Their work helps us understand and enjoy the Universe around us.

Stellar astronomer
American Annie Jump Cannon started work at Harvard College Observatory, USA, in 1896. Astronomers were then working hard to understand the nature of stars. Cannon studied the spectra of over a quarter of a million stars. She developed a system of grouping the stars into types according to their spectra. Her system is still used today.

Space astronomers
Since the 1950s, astronomers have been designing and launching spacecraft to help them with their work. Astronomers from the USA and Europe work together with data collected by the Hubble Space Telescope.

Cosmologist

Englishman Fred Hoyle (above) was one of the most important astronomers of the 20th century. One of his greatest achievements was to show how chemical elements are produced inside stars. He also worked to explain the state of the Universe. He did not believe the Universe began in an explosion, but it was he who called it the 'Big Bang'.

Different types of astronomer

Astronomers who lived and worked over 100 years ago studied every object and feature of the Universe. The 21st-century astronomer is usually a specialist who studies just a part of it in great detail. Stellar astronomers are interested in the stars and what lies between them. Other astronomers concentrate on galaxies or the Solar System. Some are not concerned with objects, but specialize in the different forms of information we receive, such as radio or X-ray. Cosmologists study the origin, evolution and future of the Universe.

Astrophotographer

Astronomy and technology have always worked hand in hand. Astronomers not only design and build instruments but are quick to use the instruments and techniques of others. They have been taking astronomical photographs since the mid-19th century, soon after photography was invented. Today, astrophotographers spend their working lives producing ever-better images of the sky and the objects in it. Here, David Malin prepares to make an image using the 3.9m Anglo-Australian telescope. His photograph of the Orion Nebula lies behind.

Tools of the trade

Astronomers want to get the clearest and most detailed view possible of the stars and planets. For centuries, they relied on their eyes alone to explore the heavens. But since the invention of telescopes, they have used these instruments to look ever-further into space. Telescopes allow astronomers to see things bigger and more clearly. Like the human eye, they gather the light from a planet and process it into an image. But the lenses and mirrors they use gather much more light and produce a far more detailed image than our eyes do. Today's telescopes are enormous structures, housed inside buildings several storeys high. They take years to design and build, and are very expensive, each costing tens of millions of dollars. Countries or organizations, such as universities, join together to share the cost and then the use of a telescope.

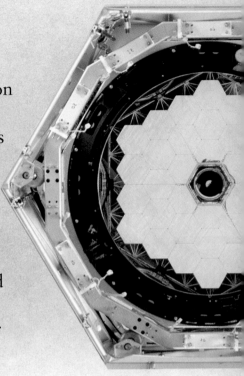

Segmented mirrors
The Keck telescopes each have a mirror measuring 10m in diameter. They are made of 36 hexagonal segments, each measuring 1.8m across.

The Kecks
Inside these domes are the Keck telescopes. Keck I has been used since 1993 and its twin, Keck II, since 1996. They are each around 25m tall and weigh around 300 tonnes.

The Subaru
The telescopes on Mauna Kea are owned and run by countries around the world. The Japanese Subaru telescope (right) can be seen inside its cylindrical dome.

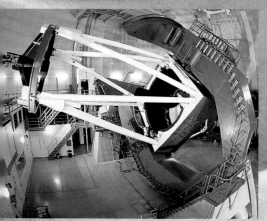

Reflecting telescopes

The world's most powerful telescopes are reflectors, which use mirrors to collect light. The bigger and better a reflector's main mirror, the more light it collects and the more information we have. The first reflectors had mirrors that could fit inside your hand. Today's are metres across. But very large mirrors bend under their own weight. The latest telescope designs use a collection of smaller mirrors arranged together to work like one big mirror. This technique means that telescopes with mirrors tens of metres across can be made. Astronomers can also use individual telescopes linked together to work like one telescope with one large mirror.

Very Large Telescope

On a mountain top at Paranal in Chile four separate telescopes have mirrors 8.2m across. Together they are known as the VLT (Very Large Telescope). Each telescope is a million times more powerful than the human eye. When linked together by computer, they are more powerful still.

City of domes

A mountain-top observatory is usually home to a number of large telescopes. Mauna Kea, a dormant volcano in Hawaii, has 12 world-class telescopes on its site, including the two Kecks which are jointly the world's largest individual telescopes. Astronomers using the instruments do not work at the eye-end of the telescopes but are usually found further down the mountain, where they use a television system and computers to record information collected by the telescopes.

Telescope mounts

Telescopes are supported on stands called mounts. A blue-painted mount (left) holds the 3.5m reflector at the Calar Alto Observatory in Spain. The mount not only takes the weight of the telescope but allows it to be positioned with ease. At the push of a button, the mount moves the telescope up and down and from side to side so it can point to anywhere in the sky. Automatic computer controls also keep the telescope tracked on an object, such as a star, as the Earth turns. Otherwise the star would quickly move out of the telescope's view.

Observatory Earth

The world's most powerful telescopes are sited on mountain tops around the globe. Several telescopes occupy the same site, together forming an observatory. The telescopes work above the clouds, far away from city lights, where the air is clear, still, dry and thin. Here, astronomers look into the darkest skies above Earth and get the best view of the Universe.

NORTH AMERICA

Owens Valley, USA

1. Mt Wilson, USA
2. Palomar, USA
3. Kitt Peak, USA
4. Mt Hopkins, USA
5. Mt Graham, USA
6. McDonald Observatory, USA

Mauna Kea Observatories, Hawaii

Green Bank, USA

Socorro, USA

Arecibo, USA

Jodrell Bank, UK
Cambridge, UK
Effelsberg, Germany
Nancay, France

Calar Alto, Spain

European Northern Observatory, La Palma

SOUTH AMERICA

7. ESO, Paranal, Chile
8. Las Campañas, Chile
9. ESO, La Silla, Chile
10. Cerro Tololo, Chile
11. Gemini Observatory, Cerro Pachon, Chile

First observatories

The first telescopes, like Galileo's, were small and light. But very soon, astronomers were using bigger and heavier ones that needed to be on permanent mounts and inside protective buildings. The first national observatories, such as the one at Greenwich, London, were built near cities in the late 17th century.

Greenwich Observatory
The telescopes of the Octagon Room at Greenwich were used to show visitors the stars and planets, while the astronomer's specialist instruments were kept elsewhere.

Mountain-top observatories

In the late 19th century, astronomers started to take advantage of the good observing conditions at remote mountain-top locations. The Lick Observatory, USA, built in the 1880s, was the first permanent mountain-top observatory. Until the 1960s, most observatories were in the northern hemisphere and the southern skies were relatively unexplored. Today, there are world-class, mountain-top observatories in the north and south.

Kitt Peak

Kitt Peak National Observatory in Arizona, USA, dates from 1958. At first, there were just two small telescopes. Today, there are 15 major telescopes, each run by an American university or government institution.

European Southern Observatory, Chile

In the 1960s, a number of European countries joined together to build the European Southern Observatory at La Silla in Chile. Additional observatories are now located on neighbouring mountain ridges.

Arecibo radio telescope

The 305m dish at Arecibo, Puerto Rico, is the largest single radio dish in the world. It is built in a natural hollow in the island's hills and faces different parts of the sky as it turns with the Earth.

ASIA

EUROPE

Mt Pastukhov, Russia

AFRICA

Hartebeesthoek, South Africa

South African Astronomical Observatory

AUSTRALIA

12

13

14

12. Narrabri, Australia
13. Anglo-Australian Observatory, Australia
14. Parkes, Australia

	Sites of major optical telescopes
	Radio telescopes

Anglo-Australian Observatory

The Anglo-Australian Observatory is funded and run by the British and Australian governments. Astronomers from both countries have been viewing the southern sky from here for about 30 years.

Invisible Universe

Our eyes let us see the stars in the sky. They collect the light waves that travel across space, and form these into images. Light is just one form of energy wave emitted by the stars – they send out others such as X-ray, infra-red and radio waves. If our eyes could collect the others, we would see so much more of the Universe. Special telescopes on the ground and in space allow astronomers to collect this extra information from the stars. Familiar objects are shown in a new way and whole objects normally invisible are revealed. Even though we have discovered more Universe by collecting the range of wavelengths, astronomers think there is much more waiting to be found.

Filling in the picture
Astronomers have been collecting the different wavelengths from space for about 40 years. Each type of wavelength is collected and studied independently, and objects look different in the various wavelengths. The Crab Nebula is the remains of a star that exploded in 1054. The infra-red view is top left, the usual light wave view is top right, and underneath are the radio (above left) and X-ray view (above right).

The search for dark matter

Astronomers believe that everything we know about is only a tiny part of the material in the Universe. As much as 95 per cent of the Universe is missing. If this material gave out light, radio, infra-red or other waves we would detect it. It does not, but we know it is there because astronomers have seen the effects of its gravity, and have identified places where some exists. They think the missing material, called dark matter, could be tiny particles smaller than atoms. One type of these particles is called WIMPs (weakly interactive massive particles). They have not been found yet, but the search is on.

Dark matter map
The computer model above shows a part of the Universe billions of kilometres wide. Dark matter (red) lies between the galaxies (blue). The dark matter's gravity bends the light (yellow) from the galaxies. If there was no dark matter, the light paths would be straight.

Collecting waves
Radio waves make it through Earth's atmosphere and are collected at sea level. Light also makes it through but is best collected at mountain-top sites, along with infra-red waves. Other wavelengths do not get through and must be collected by telescopes in space.

Listening into space
Radio astronomy began in 1932, when Karl Jansky detected radio signals from the Milky Way. A radio dish telescope collects the radio waves. They are turned into electric signals and stored on computer for use by astronomers. The Very Large Array in New Mexico, USA (left), is made of 27 dishes, each one 25m across, working as a group.

Gamma rays

X-rays

Ultraviolet

Light

Infra-red

Radio

Energy spectrum
The full range of energy waves given off by objects in space is known as the electromagnetic spectrum. The various wavelengths reveal different aspects of the Universe. Gamma rays have identified far distant, exploding stars, and X-rays have shown the location of black holes. Ultraviolet energy is given off by the hottest stars, infra-red waves reveal newly born stars normally hidden by dust, and radio waves have provided evidence for the Big Bang.

Space explorers

Many astronomers would love to go into space and see for themselves what it is like. Although men travelled to the Moon in the years 1969 to 1972 and people now regularly spend time in space around Earth, we are not ready to go any further. So, astronomers stay on Earth and send spacecraft to explore and study the Universe on their behalf. Spacecraft do not need to eat or sleep or return home once their work is done. Astronomers use two types of craft – spaceprobes and space telescopes.

Exploring Mars
Many probes have been sent to study Mars. *Pathfinder* landed on its surface in July 1997. It then opened to release *Sojourner* (above), a buggy the size of a microwave oven, to drive over the Martian surface. Two larger Mars Exploration Rovers, *Spirit* and *Opportunity*, landed on the surface in 2004.

Space robots

Spaceprobes are robotic explorers sent into the Solar System. In the last 40 years or so, they have been sent to all of the Solar System planets except Pluto. They have also visited moons, comets and asteroids. A spaceprobe is about the size of a car or minibus. It has its own power, computer and communication systems, cameras and a set of experiments and instruments for investigating its target. Each probe is designed for a particular mission. It might fly by its target (such as a planet or moon), go into orbit round it or land on it.

Launch to space

Spaceprobes and satellites are launched into space by rockets. The *Ariane* rocket (left) launches European satellites and probes into space from its launch site at Kourou, French Guiana, South America.

Journey to Saturn

Even after a spaceprobe is launched it can be years before it starts work. The *Cassini* spacecraft faced a seven-year journey after its launch to Saturn in October 1997. Its instruments were switched on while it flew by Jupiter, but the craft only became fully operational once it reached Saturn in 2004.

Investigating Titan

Cassini carried a small probe called *Huygens* (below). *Huygens* investigated the atmosphere and surface of Titan, Saturn's largest moon, in January 2005.

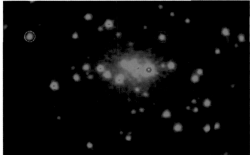

X-ray view

Astronomers hope that *XMM-Newton* will help them understand more about distant objects such as galaxies and black holes. This is an X-ray view of the central region of the Andromeda Galaxy.

Eyes on the Universe

Space telescopes are a type of satellite which look out into space as they orbit around Earth. Astronomers have been looking at the Universe with space telescopes for about 40 years. They work in much the same way as Earth-based telescopes, by collecting and recording information from space objects. Some are working above us now. Their advantage is that they are above Earth's atmosphere and weather. This means they can work 24 hours a day, 365 days a year, and they can collect wavelengths that do not travel through the atmosphere, such as X-rays.

XMM-Newton

The *XMM-Newton* space telescope has been collecting X-rays since December 1999. The X-rays are collected by sets of wafer-thin mirrors nested within the telescope's three barrel-shaped entrances.

THE SOLAR SYSTEM

Earth belongs to a family of planets, moons, comets and spacerocks, all of which orbit around the Sun. As a group these objects are called the Solar System. They have been together for around 4,600 million years, when they were made from a giant spinning cloud of gas and dust. The Sun was the first to form, in the centre of the cloud. Surrounding it was a spinning disc of leftover material, which over millions of years formed into the nine planets. The Sun is the most massive member of the Solar System and has the biggest gravitational pull. The Sun's gravity keeps the group together.

Moving worlds
All the objects in the Solar System travel around the Sun. A complete circuit is called an orbit. Each object rotates as it follows its orbit.

Rock planets
Mercury, Venus, Earth, Mars and Pluto are the rock planets. They started as tiny particles of dust and gas, which clumped together to form larger and larger particles, then lumps, boulders and finally giant spheres of rock – the planets.

Solar System model
In the past, people learned about the Solar System from models like this orrery (below). Its planets revolve around the central Sun.

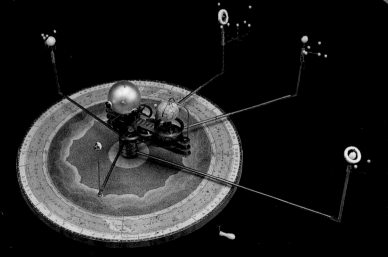

Mercury
Mercury is the closest planet to the Sun and orbits it the fastest.

Venus
Venus is the slowest spinning planet. It is also the hottest, with a thick atmosphere.

Earth
Earth has liquid water on its surface. Nearer the Sun, water would boil; further away it would freeze.

Observing the planets
Five planets – Mercury, Venus, Mars, Jupiter and Saturn – are easy to see with the naked eye, if you know where to look! Planets are disc-shaped, unlike stars which appear as pinpoints of bright light. Usually, only one or two planets are visible in the same part of the sky. Occasionally, more can be lined up in the sky, as here in the early evening of May 2002.

Distant gas giants
Jupiter, Saturn, Uranus and Neptune do not have solid surfaces like the rock planets. What we see is the top of a gas giant's atmosphere.

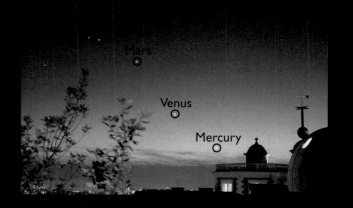

Moons and spacerocks
Seven of the planets have moons – rocky bodies which orbit around the planets like mini solar systems. There are at least 100 moons in our Solar System. The largest is bigger than Mercury and the smallest are hill-sized, potato-shaped lumps. Billions of spacerocks, called asteroids, orbit the Sun between Mars and Jupiter. Further out, nearer Neptune and Pluto, are icy spacerocks, the Kuiper Belt objects. Way beyond are trillions of comets that form the vast, spherical Oort Cloud.

Mars	**Jupiter**	**Saturn**	**Uranus**	**Neptune**	**Pluto**
Mars is about half the size of Earth and spins around once in about the same time, just over 24½ hours.	Jupiter is the largest and most massive planet, and also the fastest spinner. It spins around in under ten hours.	Saturn is the second largest planet. It is nearly ten times as far away from the Sun as Earth.	Uranus' rings appear to go over its top rather than around its middle. This is because it is tilted on its side.	Neptune is the smallest, most distant of the gas giants. It is 30 times as far from the Sun as Earth.	Pluto is the most distant and smallest planet – smaller than Earth's Moon. Its orbit takes nearly 248 years.

The Sun

The Sun is a vast ball of incredibly hot, brilliant gas. It measures 1.4 million km across – 109 Earths could fit across its face. It contains over 99 per cent of all the material in the Solar System. Like other stars, the Sun is not a solid object, but we can detect a visible surface called the photosphere. The temperature here is 5,500°C. The Sun shines because it produces light energy. It has been shining for around 4,600 million years and will continue for the next 5,000 million years or so.

Sunspots and flares

The photosphere is a busy and violent place. Gas is constantly swirling and shooting up from the surface in jets, columns and sheets. Dark spots, hundreds or thousands of kilometres wide, regularly appear and gigantic gas flares arch over them.

The Sun's atmosphere

Beyond its bright and hectic surface is the Sun's atmosphere, stretching for millions of kilometres into space. The inner atmosphere, the chromosphere (above), and the outer one, the corona, are not normally visible from Earth. But during a total solar eclipse, the Sun's atmosphere is revealed.

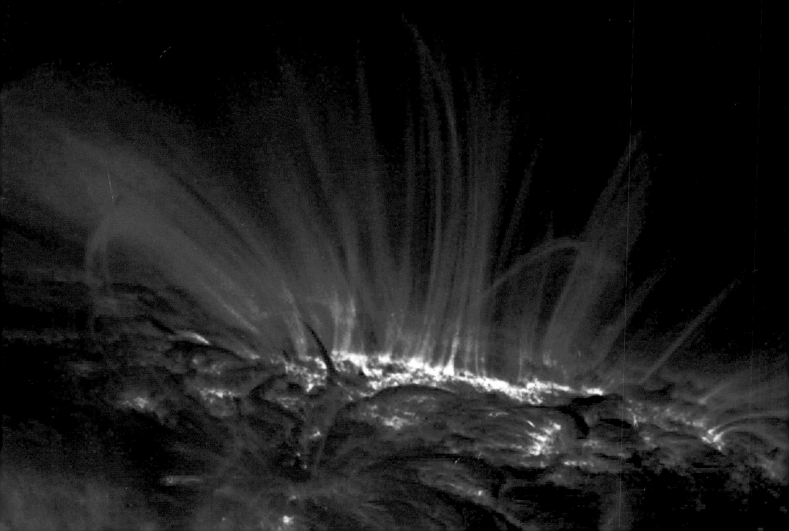

Inside the Sun

About three quarters of the Sun is hydrogen. The rest is mainly helium with tiny amounts of other elements. Gravity keeps the gas together, pulling it in towards the Sun's centre, and stopping it from drifting off into space. In the centre, the gas is packed together and gets much hotter. About 60 per cent of the Sun's gas is squashed into the core, where temperatures are an incredible 15 million °C. Here in the core, hydrogen is converted into helium, producing huge amounts of energy. Every second, about 600 million tons of hydrogen is converted. The energy zigzags its way slowly to the surface where it leaves the Sun, mostly as light and heat.

Light display

Occasionally, in areas near Earth's poles, skywatchers can view spectacular light shows. This is the aurora borealis, or northern lights, seen here above Alaska.

Discovering helium

Helium was discovered in the Sun before it was found on Earth. English astronomer Norman Lockyer was looking at a spectrum of the Sun's light in 1868. He saw a line across the spectrum, which could not have been produced by any of the elements known on Earth. He realized it was made by a new element. He called it helium from the Greek word for the Sun, *helios*.

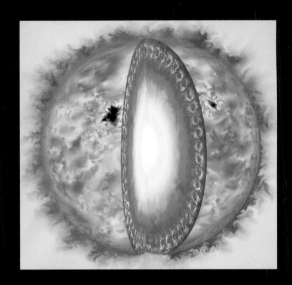

Looking at the Sun

The Sun is a familiar sight from Earth. But no one should look directly at the Sun. Its intense light can damage our eyes. Astronomers investigate the Sun by using specialist telescopes to record its details, which they study later. Yet there are some solar displays we can watch, such as an aurora, a show of colourful rays and streamers in the sky. This occurs when the solar wind, made of incredibly tiny particles, spirals out from the Sun and travels far into space, journeying past the planets and out of the Solar System. As the wind streams past Earth, some of its particles enter our atmosphere and become trapped by magnetic lines around Earth's poles. They collide with air molecules, which glow and create the aurora.

Earth: home planet

Earth is the biggest rock planet and the third one from the Sun. It is 12,756km across. Every part of it is special to us, providing us with everything we need to survive. Anyone visiting Earth from another planet would see that our buildings, crops and roads make their mark on Earth. Yet, the same visitor would see a planet covered largely by water, with land masses which change appearance by natural forces. He would experience temperatures from an icy -90°C to a searing 58°C, see dry, arid land and lush vegetation, and find life wherever he looked. Each 23.9-hour turn of the Earth brings night and day, and every 365.25-day year, as the Earth orbits the Sun, brings the seasons.

Eye on Earth
We still have much to learn about Earth. We investigate it from the ground and by using satellites in space. Satellites monitor such things as Earth's climate, its polar ice caps, the growth of crops and ocean currents.

Life
Earth is the only planet where life is known to exist. It is found all around the globe – on every continent, in its oceans and flying through its air.

Water cycle
Water moves constantly between the planet and its atmosphere. In this rainforest, rain has fallen and mist is rising. It will condense into clouds and rain will fall once more.

Explosive Earth
Earth's outer shell is broken into pieces called plates. These move against and away from each other causing earthquakes and volcanic eruptions such as that of Mount Etna in Sicily.

Changing face
Some changes to the Earth are immediate, others happen slowly. Both air and water can slowly erode Earth's surface. Wind has sculpted rocks in the Utah Desert in the USA, and the Greenland ice sheet erodes land as it moves.

Blue planet

From space, it is easy to see that water covers most of Earth's surface, a total of 71%. Water gives our planet its distinctive colour. Also visible is some of the atmosphere which surrounds Earth. This is the thin layer of gas, rich in nitrogen, which protects Earth from harmful energy waves, maintains a safe temperature range and provides the air we breathe. In the 1860s, the English scientist James Glaisher made 28 daring balloon ascents to study the atmosphere. He and his companion flew to altitudes of around 10km, where the atmosphere is so thin they almost lost their lives.

Earth's land
Africa is visible here below Earth's clouds. It is one of the planet's seven land masses, or continents.

Earth's Moon

The Moon is our closest neighbour in space. It orbits around us at a distance of 384,500km and journeys with Earth as it makes its yearly orbit around the Sun. It is a cold, lifeless ball of rock about a quarter of the size of Earth. It has no atmosphere or liquid water, and its dusty surface is covered in hollows called craters. The Moon is by far the largest object in the night sky and shines brightly by reflected sunlight. It has been studied by astronomers for thousands of years, and is the only place outside Earth that humans have visited.

The same face

Only one side of the Moon is ever visible from Earth. It is called the nearside. This is because the Moon spins around once in the same amount of time that it takes to orbit once around Earth. See how the same side (marked by a dot) always faces Earth but spins and orbits in a 27.3-day period.

The Moon's phases

The Moon seems to change its shape gradually from day to day. It is not really changing. The nearside of the Moon is always facing us, but we see only the part lit by the Sun. When the Moon's nearside is unlit, it is virtually invisible. This is called New Moon. When the nearside is fully lit it is Full Moon. Each different shape is a phase of the Moon. One complete cycle, from New Moon to New Moon, takes 29.5 days.

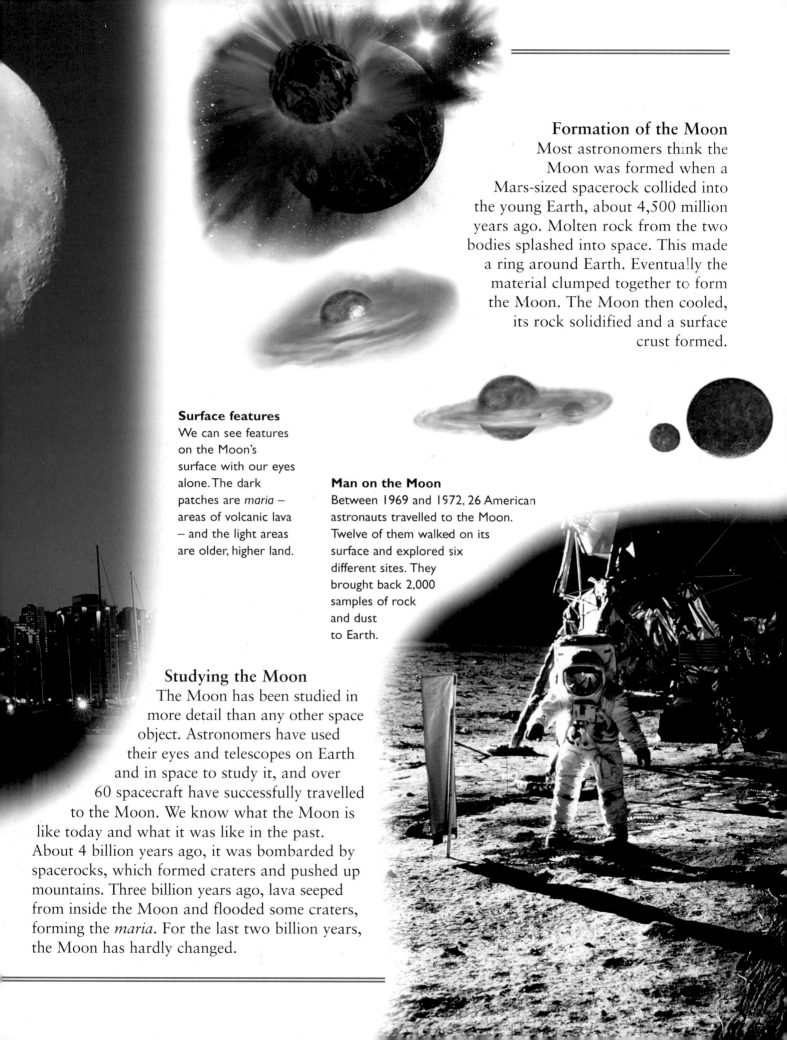

Formation of the Moon

Most astronomers think the Moon was formed when a Mars-sized spacerock collided into the young Earth, about 4,500 million years ago. Molten rock from the two bodies splashed into space. This made a ring around Earth. Eventually the material clumped together to form the Moon. The Moon then cooled, its rock solidified and a surface crust formed.

Surface features

We can see features on the Moon's surface with our eyes alone. The dark patches are *maria* – areas of volcanic lava – and the light areas are older, higher land.

Man on the Moon

Between 1969 and 1972, 26 American astronauts travelled to the Moon. Twelve of them walked on its surface and explored six different sites. They brought back 2,000 samples of rock and dust to Earth.

Studying the Moon

The Moon has been studied in more detail than any other space object. Astronomers have used their eyes and telescopes on Earth and in space to study it, and over 60 spacecraft have successfully travelled to the Moon. We know what the Moon is like today and what it was like in the past. About 4 billion years ago, it was bombarded by spacerocks, which formed craters and pushed up mountains. Three billion years ago, lava seeped from inside the Moon and flooded some craters, forming the *maria*. For the last two billion years, the Moon has hardly changed.

Rock worlds

Mercury and Pluto are the two smallest planets in the Solar System. Pluto is tiny, at 2,270km across, and Mercury is 4,880km – one smaller and one bigger than Earth's Moon. Each is a sphere of rock, but they are worlds of opposites. Mercury is the closest planet to the Sun and gets incredibly hot. It is the fastest orbiter of all the planets, travelling around the Sun once every 88 days. Pluto is the most distant planet, 100 times further from the Sun than Mercury, and is a desolate, frozen world. It is the slowest orbiter and takes nearly 248 years to travel around the Sun. Both planets are difficult to see from Earth and are largely unknown.

Seeing Mercury

Mercury is hard to observe because it is never far from the Sun in our sky. In the 1920s, French astronomer Eugène Antoniadi drew maps of markings he observed on its surface. In 1974 we saw what Mercury is really like when the first pictures were transmitted to Earth by *Mariner 10*.

Hot and cold

It is scorching hot on the part of Mercury facing the Sun – around 450°C, much hotter than a kitchen oven. But the temperature plunges to a freezing cold -180°C at night because Mercury has such a thin atmosphere, far too thin to hold in the heat.

Mercury, cratered world

Mercury is a dry, cratered, dead world whose surface has hardly changed in millions of years. Its craters were formed when the young planet was bombarded by spacerocks and its plains were formed when lava flooded the surface. Only one spaceprobe, *Mariner 10*, has visited Mercury so far. It flew by the planet three times in 1974–75. Astronomers are now set to return. The United States' *Messenger* probe will fly by Mercury in 2008 and 2009 and a European probe called *BepiColombo* will be launched in 2012.

Pluto from Earth

Pluto was discovered in 1930 and its one moon, Charon, which is about half Pluto's size, in 1978. Even the powerful Hubble Space Telescope cannot give us detailed views of these worlds. Looking at Pluto is like trying to look at a golf ball 100km away.

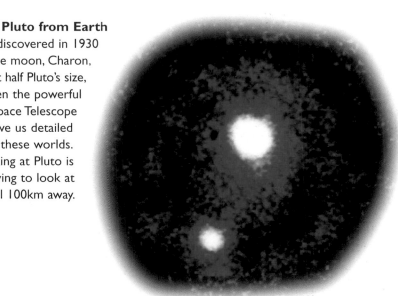

Discovery

American astronomer Clyde Tombaugh discovered Pluto from the Lowell Observatory in Arizona, USA. Night after night he took photographs of the starry sky. Pluto appeared as a dot which moved position from image to image compared with stars, which are stationary.

Pluto – odd planet out

Remote Pluto is the planet we know least about. Its distance and size make it difficult to observe, and it is the only planet not yet explored by spaceprobe. Astronomers hope to change this and are planning to get a mission to Pluto by 2020. From Earth we can tell Pluto is very different from its neighbours. Its size, structure and composition are nothing like those of the gas giants. It also has a strange orbit, which is the least circular of all the planets' orbits and has the biggest tilt. These differences make some astronomers think Pluto is not a planet but a large icy object belonging to the Kuiper Belt.

Pluto's path

Pluto's strange orbit is shown above in green. For about 20 years of each orbit Pluto is within Neptune's orbit and is closer to the Sun than Neptune is.

Distant worlds

In this artist's impression we see Pluto in the sky above Charon. In the distance is the Sun. Pluto is too far from the Sun to receive any obvious light or heat. Its temperature is around -220°C and its surface is permanently frozen.

Near neighbours

Venus and Mars are Earth's closest planetary neighbours. All three are spheres of rock, but they are very different on the surface. Venus, which is nearer to the Sun than Earth, is a hot, suffocating world. The temperature on Venus builds up to an incredible 464°C, while the highest temperature recorded on Earth is about 57.8°C. Mars lies further away from the Sun and is cold and barren. The temperature at its poles is an icy -120°C. Both Venus and Mars are easy to see in Earth's sky, and they have been observed by astronomers for thousands of years. But we have only known what they are really like since spacecraft went to take a closer look.

Slow spinner
Venus spins more slowly than any of the other planets – once every 243 days. This is longer than the time it takes to orbit the Sun. Its clouds spin around the planet much faster. They are mainly carbon dioxide and they trap the Sun's heat, helping to make Venus such a hot place.

View from Earth
Venus is easy to spot from Earth, but its thick, cloudy atmosphere stops us from observing its surface. It also stops most of the sunlight shining on Venus from reaching the ground, making Venus a very gloomy place.

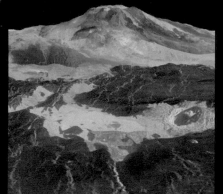

Volcanic surface
Astronomers got their first good look under Venus' clouds in 1975 when a spaceprobe survived its journey through the atmosphere and sent back an image of a rocky surface. More recently, astronomers have used radar to see through the clouds to the surface below. In the early 1990s, *Magellan* (above) used radar to map nearly all of Venus's surface. It showed a rocky landscape formed by volcanic activity. There are huge volcanoes and lava flows all over Venus. Over 150 volcanoes are more than 100km wide. Maat Mons (left) is one of the biggest. It measures 200km across and 8km high.

Investigating Mars

Mars has always fascinated people. It is a rock planet like our own and, after Earth, is the world most likely to support life. Books and films have told of fantastic creatures living on Mars and imagined Martians invading Earth. Astronomers have been sending spaceprobes to Mars over the past 40 years to find out what the planet is really like. Probes have orbited the planet, have landed on it and robotic vehicles have driven across its surface. They have made detailed maps of the planet, studied its weather and tested its rocks for signs of life.

Studying Mars
Percival Lowell studied Mars from his observatory in Arizona, USA, in the 1890s. He mistakenly believed he could see canals on the surface that must have been dug by an intelligent life form living on Mars.

A day on Mars
Mars is about half the size of Earth and one-and-a-half times further from the Sun. It spins around once in just over 24½ hours and so its day length is very similar to Earth's.

The red planet
Mars has a very thin atmosphere and so we can usually look straight at its reddish surface. It is called the red planet because it appears red in Earth's sky. Its colour comes from iron oxide (rust) in the planet's soil.

Rocky landscape
The surface of Mars is like a huge, frozen, rocky desert peppered with volcanoes much larger than anything on Earth. Olympus Mons (left), the largest volcano in the Solar System, stands 24km high and 600km across. A vast canyon system, the Valles Marineris (below), measuring 4,000km from end to end and up to 7km deep, cuts across the planet.

35

Spacerocks

There are billions of lumps of rock in the Solar System. These are the asteroids. Over 90 per cent of them are found in a doughnut-shaped ring between the orbits of Mars and Jupiter. Astronomers have known about the asteroids here, in the Main Belt, ever since they discovered Ceres in 1801. They know now of a second belt of icy spacerocks, the Kuiper Belt, at the edge of the planetary Solar System. The first of these was discovered in September 1992. Astronomers study asteroids in space and others down on Earth.

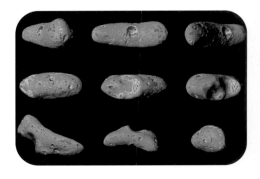

Eros
Eros has been studied in greater detail than any other asteroid. The spaceprobe *NEAR* took images of Eros from different angles before landing on it in February 2001. The images are coloured to help scientists study Eros's surface and structure.

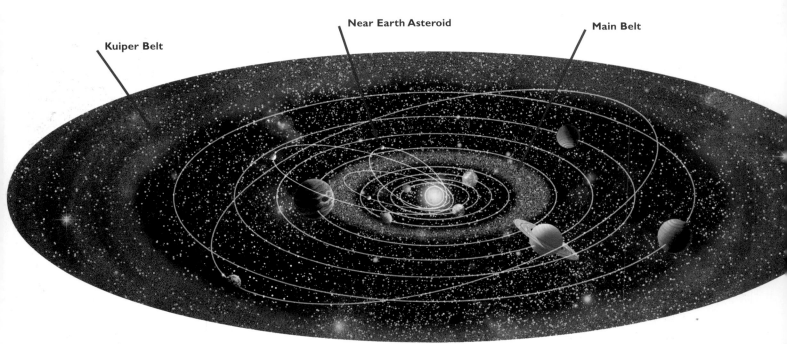

Kuiper Belt   Near Earth Asteroid   Main Belt

Asteroids
Asteroids are rocky material that was left over when the planets and moons were formed 4,600 million years ago. They come in a range of sizes, from boulder and mountain-sized to the biggest, Ceres, at 933km across. All but the largest are irregular in shape, like potatoes. Each takes just a few years for its orbit around the Sun, and spins as it travels, turning once in hours or weeks. Some asteroids are not in the Main Belt, but follow orbits that bring them close to Earth's orbit. These are the Near Earth Asteroids – Eros is one.

Ida and Gaspra
Ida (right) has a tiny moon of its own, called Dactyl. Gaspra (far right) measures 12km across, and is found near the inner edge of the Main Belt.

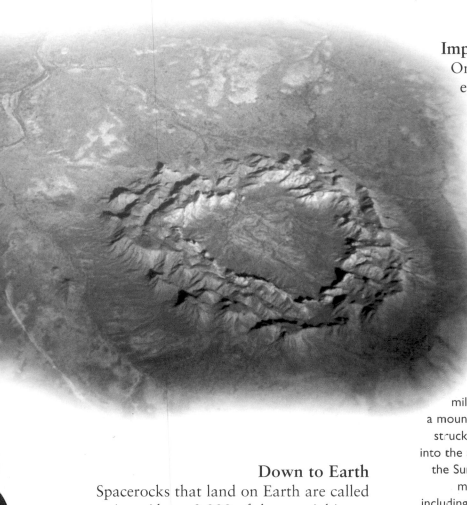

Impact with Earth

On every continent on Earth there is evidence that asteroids have collided into our planet. An asteroid crashing into Earth produces a crater. The size of the crater depends on the size of the colliding rock. There are about 160 craters on Earth. Most of these were formed more than 100 million years ago. The Wolfe Creek Crater in Australia (left) is 870m across and was formed around 300,000 years ago.

Chicxulub

The Chicxulub Crater was formed about 65 million years ago, when a mountain-sized spacerock struck Earth. Material sent into the atmosphere blocked the Sun's heat and light for months, and most life, including the dinosaurs, died.

Down to Earth

Spacerocks that land on Earth are called meteorites. About 3,000 of them weighing over 1kg each land every year. Most fall into the sea, the rest hit land. Scientists hunt for meteorites in the undisturbed and barren regions of Earth. Most of the thousands of meteorites that have been found are pieces of asteroids. But over 20 arrived here from the Moon and over 20 more from Mars.

Meteorite hunt

Antarctica is a great place to hunt for meteorites. The dark rocks are easy to spot on the ice (below). Once collected, thin slices of the meteorite can be studied closely (left).

The King

Jupiter is a huge planet – the biggest in the Solar System. It has the largest family of moons and is the fastest spinner, turning around once in less than ten hours. Jupiter is a freezing cold -110°C at its surface, but an amazing 30,000°C in its core. It was the first of the giant planets to be visited by spacecraft when *Pioneer 10* flew by it in 1973. Since then the two *Voyagers* and the *Galileo* probe have investigated the planet.

Great Red Spot
The main feature of Jupiter's surface is the Great Red Spot, an enormous hurricane over twice the size of Earth. Astronomers have been watching this storm change appearance for over 300 years.

Inside Jupiter

Jupiter is made mostly of hydrogen, the element that stars are made from, with some helium. If Jupiter had been made of about 50 times more hydrogen, it would have turned into a star. Jupiter does not have a solid surface but a 1,000km-deep shell of hydrogen and helium gas, its atmosphere. Below this outer layer is liquid hydrogen and helium. Deep inside is a solid core.

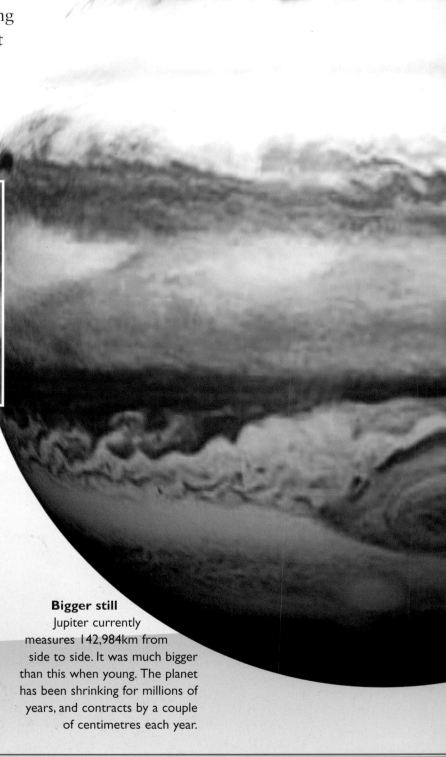

Bigger still
Jupiter currently measures 142,984km from side to side. It was much bigger than this when young. The planet has been shrinking for millions of years, and contracts by a couple of centimetres each year.

Stormy weather

When we look at Jupiter we look at the top layer of its atmosphere. This is made of different coloured bands. The bright ones, called zones, are rising gas. The darker ones, called belts, are falling gas. Jupiter's rapid spin, coupled with the rising heat from inside the planet, create atmospheric turbulence, super-fast winds and raging storms.

King of the planets
When early astronomers named Jupiter, they did not know it was the largest planet. But they must have seen that it is one of the brightest objects in the sky. They named it after the king of the Roman gods.

View from Earth
Jupiter is hundreds of millions of kilometres from Earth, but is easy to spot in our sky. It reflects the Sun's light well and looks like a bright silver star to our eyes. The bands across its surface and the four largest of its moons can be seen through a small telescope.

Bigger than Earth
Earth is tiny in comparison with Jupiter. Eleven Earths could fit across Jupiter's face and 1,300 Earths could fit inside the huge planet.

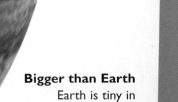

Spaceprobe exploration
The *Galileo* probe has been the most successful craft to explore Jupiter. It arrived at the planet in 1995 and spent eight years investigating Jupiter and its moons. The probe's last job was to plunge into Jupiter's atmosphere before the planet's strong gravity ripped it apart.

Jupiter

Saturn

Ringed worlds

The four largest planets in the Solar System – Jupiter, Saturn, Uranus and Neptune – have much in common. They are all distant, cold and colourful worlds whose outer surfaces are made of gas, and all have rings surrounding them. They are all made mainly of hydrogen, but other elements in their outer layers give them their distinctive colour. The rings of all four planets look solid from a distance. But when seen in close-up, it is clear they are made of billions of individual pieces of rock, which orbit around their parent planet like tiny moons.

Clear view
The Dutch astronomer Christiaan Huygens observed Saturn and worked out that the planet had a ring of material around it. He published his theory in 1655.

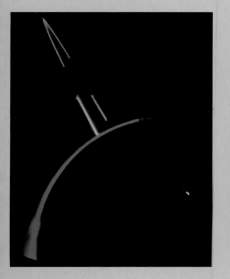

Jupiter's ring
Jupiter's faint ring system was discovered by the *Voyager 1* spaceprobe in 1979. It is made up of a handful of rings formed from dust pieces. The dust was knocked off the planet's inner moons in Jupiter's past.

Lord of the rings
When Galileo looked at Saturn in 1610, he spotted something at either side of the planet. Saturn seemed to have 'ears'. Galileo thought these must be moons. But during the 1650s, Christiaan Huygens observed Saturn when the planet was further along its orbit. He was able to make out a ring surrounding the planet. Both Galileo and Huygens had seen Saturn's main rings (illustrated top). In fact, Saturn has many more rings than this. There are very faint rings inside the main system and many more stretching way beyond, about four times as far from the planet.

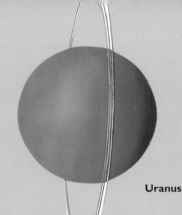

Uranus

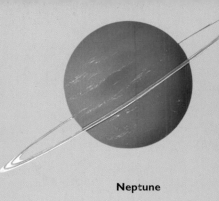

Neptune

Changing view

As Saturn moves around the Sun on its orbit, we see its rings from different angles. Twice each orbit the rings are edge on to us and almost impossible to see. For the remainder of the time we see a varying amount of them, from above or below.

Changing Neptune

A giant cloud system, the Great Dark Spot, was discovered on Neptune's surface by *Voyager 2* in 1989. But it had disappeared by the time the Hubble Space Telescope was pointed at Neptune just five years later.

Discovering Uranus and Neptune

Until 1781, astronomers believed Saturn was the most distant planet. In that year, English astronomer William Herschel discovered Uranus, which is over twice as far from the Sun as Saturn. Its ring system was discovered in 1977. Neptune was discovered by German astronomer Johann Galle in 1846. Much of our knowledge of these two faraway planets came from the one probe that has visited them. This was *Voyager 2* in the 1980s. It provided close-up views and discovered Neptune's ring and moons around both of the planets.

Rings in close-up

Saturn has a complex ring system. The rings are made up of hundreds of ringlets. Each of these is made of chunks of icy rock and dust, which follow individual orbits around Saturn. The main rings are made of chunks the size of a house; the fainter rings are made of smaller, pebble-sized ones.

Uranus and family

It is difficult to observe Uranus because of its great distance from us. Today's large Earth-based telescopes, however, reveal its ring system and larger moons. From left to right the moons pictured here are: Titania, Umbriel, Miranda, Ariel and Oberon.

Planetary moons

There are over 100 moons in the Solar System. Between them they orbit around seven of the planets – only Mercury and Venus have no moon. The smallest moons are the size of a small town and the largest are bigger than the smallest planets. Until 30 years ago we knew of only 33 moons, but more were discovered when the two *Voyager* spaceprobes flew by the ringed planets in the 1980s. Since then, more powerful telescopes and improved techniques mean that we are discovering more and more.

Origins
Jupiter has the largest family of moons. Sixty-three have been identified and astronomers are looking for more. The larger moons, such as Ganymede, were formed when Jupiter was made. Its smaller moons are asteroids, captured by Jupiter's gravity. Mars has two asteroid moons, Phobos and Deimos.

Saturn's moons
Astronomers have identified 34 moons orbiting Saturn, and there are probably more. Like most other moons in the Solar System, they are named after figures from ancient mythology. Tethys (above right) and Dione (above left) are named after two sisters of the god Saturn.

Ganymede and Janus
Jupiter's Ganymede (left) is the largest of all the Solar System moons. It is 5,262km wide – bigger than Mercury and Pluto. Saturn's Janus (right), at 191km across, is a small moon. Even smaller ones, 2-3km across, are known.

Discovering moons

The first moons to be discovered, apart from Earth's Moon, were found around Jupiter and Saturn in the 17th century. The Italian-French astronomer Giovanni Cassini (left) made a study of Saturn and discovered Iapetus, Rhea, Tethys and Dione, as well as the gap in Saturn's ring that is named after him. The first of Uranus's 27 moons was discovered in 1787, and Triton, the largest of Neptune's 13 known moons, in 1846. Pluto's only moon, Charon, was detected in 1978.

Closer investigation

Spaceprobes have shown us what many of the moons are like. Each is a rock or rock and ice body. The small, irregular-shaped ones look much the same. But the large, round ones have vastly different features. There are ice volcanoes, frozen oceans, sulphur spurts, red hot lava and grooved and cratered surfaces. The *Cassini* mission will reveal more about Saturn's moons, particularly Titan (left), which is the only moon with a substantial atmosphere. Its surface is beneath thick, moving orange clouds.

Io and Europa

Io and Europa, two of Jupiter's larger moons, are contrasting worlds. Io (below left) is covered in volcanoes, molten rock and sulphur lakes. Gas eruptions and flowing lava are happening there all the time. Europa's surface (below right) is icy smooth. Underneath the ice is a liquid ocean, which might be home to some form of life.

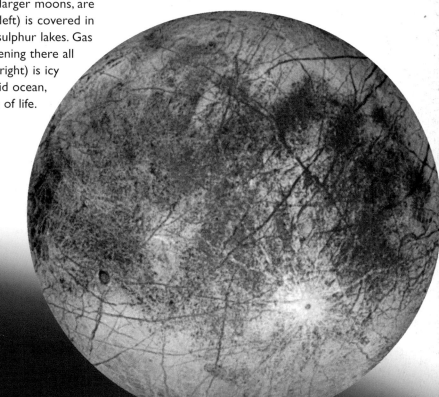

Ice kingdoms

There are about ten trillion comets in the Solar System. Each one is a mountain-sized world of snow, ice and dust – a giant cosmic snowball. Together, they make a vast sphere called the Oort Cloud, which surrounds the planetary part of the Solar System. The cloud's nearest edge is about 600,000 million km away, and its furthest about 7 million million km from us. Even the closest comets are too small and distant to be seen. It is only when a comet leaves the cloud and travels in towards the Sun that we can see it.

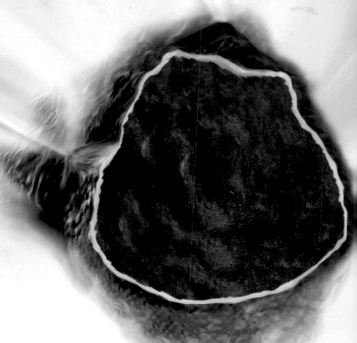

Halley's nucleus
We have seen the nucleus of only two comets. The first was that of Halley's Comet (left). The spaceprobe *Giotto* flew to within 600km of the 16km-long snowball nucleus in March 1986.

Cosmic snowball
Comets are often described as dirty snowballs, because they are lumps of snow and rocky dust. They are not in fact ball-shaped but irregular in shape, more like a potato or peanut. A slice through one would show that a layer of dust covers the snowy interior.

Fear of comets
For centuries, the sudden appearance of a comet in the sky was thought to be a sign of a coming disaster. Montezuma II, the last emperor of the Aztec people, took the arrival of this comet (below) and another brilliant comet as an omen that he would lose his empire. In 1519, he did.

Understanding comets
The first step in understanding comets came in 1705, when English astronomer Edmond Halley showed that a comet can return again and again to Earth's sky. In 1951, American astronomer Fred Whipple proposed the idea that a cometary nucleus is like a dirty snowball. He was proved right when *Giotto* investigated Halley's Comet in 1986. The *Deep Impact* craft carried a probe, which crashed into comet Tempel-1 in 2005, releasing debris from the surface. *Deep Impact*'s studies of this material will add to our knowledge of comets.

In Earth's sky

Once in a while, a comet leaves the Oort Cloud and follows a path into the inner Solar System. When the comet is closer to the Sun than Mars, the Sun's warmth turns its snow to gas. This forms a large head, called a coma, around the nucleus. Gas and dust are swept away from the nucleus and form tails. The comet is now large enough and bright enough to be seen from Earth. About 750 such comets have been seen so far. The blue gas tail and whiter dust tail of Comet Hale-Bopp (right) were clearly visible as it travelled across our sky in 1997.

Returning comets

About 150 comets follow orbits that return them to our skies in a period of less than 200 years. A new coma and tails develop each time one travels close to the Sun. They then shrink after a couple of months as the comet moves away. The coma can be 100,000km across and the tails 100 million km long.

Shooting stars

The dust lost by a comet as it travels close to the Sun is scattered along the comet's orbital path. It forms a meteoroid stream, a ring of tiny dust particles no bigger than grains of sand. As Earth travels around the Sun it passes through about 20 meteoroid streams each year. When a meteoroid enters Earth's atmosphere it heats up and produces a trail of light in our sky, a meteor. Meteors are commonly called shooting stars because that is how they appear in our sky.

Shower of light

The Leonid meteor shower is seen in November each year as Earth passes through the dust stream of Comet Tempel-Tuttle. This image was made on 17th November 1966 when a record rate of 60,000 meteors per hour was recorded.

THE REALM OF THE STARS

The Universe is full of stars. There are billions and billions of them – more than any other type of space object. Each is a huge sphere of incredibly hot, luminous gas. A star's gravity holds the gas together. The stars differ in brightness, colour, size, age and mass. Astronomers are especially interested in mass, which is the amount of gas that makes a star. Some stars are much less massive than the Sun, others are many times more massive. Mass fixes a star's other characteristics and determines its future.

Understanding stars
English astronomer Arthur Eddington (above right) was fascinated by stars and spent much of his life in understanding how they work. In particular, he showed that a star's heat and light energy are produced by changes inside the star. He is seen here in 1933 with the scientist Albert Einstein.

Galaxies

Stars are not scattered at random through space but exist in galaxies. Each is made of huge numbers of stars and there are vast distances between them. Our local star, the Sun, is in the Milky Way Galaxy. The Andromeda Galaxy (right) is one of the nearest galaxies to ours.

Stellar life cycle

Stars are being created all the time inside galaxies. They are formed within giant clouds of gas and dust, and hundreds or thousands of stars are created together in a cluster. The stars in some clusters drift apart slowly, while those of other clusters stay packed together until they die. The most massive stars have the shortest lives, living for only a few million years. Less massive stars, such as the Sun, live much longer, for billions of years. The material of dying stars is expelled back into space. It eventually becomes part of a cloud of gas and dust, and in turn is used to create new stars.

Star brightness

From Earth we see that stars differ in brightness. But this is not a true picture as the stars are at varied distances from us. A star might appear bright just because it is close. Astronomers are interested in both the apparent brightness of stars and the real brightness. That is the luminosity, the amount of light a star produces.

Stellar recycling

Nearly 12,000 years ago a star exploded and blasted its material into space. This formed the ribbons and sheets of gas and dust we call the Vela supernova remnant. In millions or billions of years the material will be used to form new stars.

Seeing stars

There are thousands of stars in the sky that can be seen using eyes alone. In cities, only the brightest shine out, but in areas where there are no street or house lights, the sky is truly dark. Here, on a clear, moonless night, the sky is covered with stars. Imaginary patterns, called constellations, drawn around the brighter stars, help stargazers to recognize individual stars and find their way about the sky. Many show people and creatures from old myths and stories. The first were devised about 4,000 years ago by the Greeks and Babylonians. In time, Islamic and then European peoples adopted these constellations. Today, Earth's sky is divided into 88 constellations, used by stargazers around the globe.

Perseus
This Arabic constellation picture shows the Greek hero Perseus. The star Algol marks the demon's head.

Changing skies
What stars you see in the sky depends on where you are on Earth, the time of year and the time of night. These stargazers are looking up at Gemini, the twins (top left), Orion, the hunter (top centre) and Taurus, the bull (top right). They are viewing the constellations in the northern hemisphere sky during a February evening.

Bright stars

Many of the night sky's bright stars have names. The brightest of them all is Sirius in the constellation Canis Major, the great dog. Its name comes from the Greek word for 'scorching'. Other names, such as Algol in the constellation Perseus, are Arabic in origin. Algol comes from the Arabic for 'demon's head'. In Greek myth, Perseus cut off the head of the gorgon Medusa and he is shown holding it in his hand.

Scorpius

Scorpius, the scorpion, is a zodiac constellation and one of the first to be devised. In Greek mythology, this is the scorpion that used its sting to kill Orion. It can be seen from the southern hemisphere and from the lower latitudes of the northern hemisphere.

Hercules

Hercules is the fifth largest constellation, visible from all but the most southerly of Earth's land. Hercules was the Greek hero who carried out 12 tasks. One was to kill a dragon, and Hercules is shown with his foot on the head of the dragon, the constellation Draco.

Phoenix

Many of the constellations in the southern sky were devised only after navigators and explorers sailed south. Phoenix was one of 12 invented by two Dutch navigators at the end of the 16th century. This constellation is best seen from the southern hemisphere.

Crux

Crux, the southern cross, is the smallest constellation in the sky, but is easy to see. Its stars were once part of Centaurus, the centaur, and were only formed into Crux in the late 16th century. Southern hemisphere stargazers will find Crux in the Milky Way.

Giants and dwarfs

Stars fall into different types. The name of each type, such as red dwarf and blue giant, tells us about the colour, temperature and size of the star. The giants are tens of times the size of the Sun. Larger still are the supergiants, which can be up to a thousand times bigger than the Sun. Stars such as the Sun are called Main Sequence stars, and these are all dwarfs. Other types of dwarfs are tiny in comparison.

Brown dwarf
New stars are forming in the pillars of gas and dust of the Eagle Nebula. Those formed of too little mass never produce light and heat. These are the brown dwarfs.

Star types
Early in the 20th century, astronomers were studying the connection between a star's characteristics. Two astronomers, working independently, Danish Ejnar Hertzsprung (above left) and American Henry Russell (above right), realized that stars fall into different types – giants and dwarfs – depending on their temperature and luminosity.

White dwarf

A white dwarf is a dying star. It has run out of gas to convert and will soon stop producing light and heat. All that is left for it now is to slowly cool and shrink. Its material gets more and more densely packed as it shrinks to about the size of Earth.

Changing stars

Most stars are made mainly of hydrogen and helium gas. Deep inside a star, the hydrogen is converted into helium in a process called nuclear fusion. Energy, such as heat and light, is produced in the process. In some stars the helium is then converted to other elements such as oxygen and carbon. A star changes its size and colour as it uses up one gas and moves on to convert another. This means a star can be both a giant and a dwarf in its lifetime and move through a range of colours.

Red supergiant

Betelgeuse, in the constellation of Orion, is a red supergiant star. All stars are incredibly hot, but a red star is one of the coolest. It is only about 3,000°C. The Sun and other yellow stars are hotter, around 5,500°C. Blue stars, which are the hottest of all, are around 30,000°C.

The Sun's future

Eventually, the Sun will become a planetary nebula (5). It will start to die as it sheds material from its outer layers. The remaining material will pack together to make a star about the size of the Earth – a white dwarf (6).

The Sun today

The Sun is now halfway through its time as a Main Sequence star (3). It will stay like this for about 5 billion years more. As its hydrogen is used up the Sun will expand and its surface cool and turn red. It will be a red giant, up to 100 times bigger (4).

The Sun's beginnings

The Sun, like other stars, was created inside a large cloud of gas and dust. It formed from cloud material collecting together (1). The material in the young Sun's centre was tightly packed and hot. When it reached 10 million °C, nuclear fusion started. Energy was produced and the Sun started to shine (2).

6

5

4

3

2

1

Explosive finish

Stars can take billions of years to die or can end their lives suddenly. The way each star dies is not by chance. Its end has been certain from the start of its life. A star's death, like the course of its life, is determined by its mass, the amount of material it is made of. Stars with much more mass than the Sun end their lives in spectacular, explosive fashion, suddenly blowing themselves apart. Stars made of less material have a slow but colourful death.

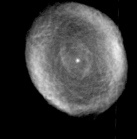

The Spirograph
All planetary nebulae have identification numbers. Some also have unofficial names. The Spirograph took its name from the drawing instrument and the patterns it creates.

The Red Spider
1,000km/s winds blast out from the white dwarf in the centre of this planetary nebula. The surrounding gas and dust glows brightly and forms a spider shape.

Bursts of colour

Stars made of less than about eight times the Sun's mass die slowly. The process starts when they push off their outer layers of gas and transform into a colourful star called a planetary nebula. They will be like this for tens of thousands of years until the material finally disperses into space. At the heart of the nebula is a white dwarf, the remains of the original star, which will cool and die over billions of years.

The Butterfly
Jets of gas burst out from the heart of this planetary nebula to form butterfly wings. There are two stars in the centre. One is a white dwarf, the remains of the red giant which pushed its outer layers into space about 1,200 years ago.

Eta Carinae

Eta Carinae is one of the most massive stars known – about 100 times more massive than the Sun. It had an explosive outburst in 1843 and was briefly the second brightest star in our sky. It is expected to die in one final explosion.

Exploding stars

Stars with more than about eight times the Sun's mass blow themselves apart. The exploding star is called a supernova and it looks like a bright new star. A core of star material is left behind. The future of this core depends on its mass. One three times the mass of the Sun produces a black hole. One with less makes a tiny, superdense neutron star, just the size of a large city.

The Cat's Eye

Today's powerful telescopes show the central star and glowing material of nebulae such as the Cat's Eye. But when the first of these stars were discovered 200 years ago, the telescopes showed them as planet-like discs. So, they were given the name planetary nebulae.

Discovery of pulsars

The Crab Nebula is the remains of a supernova that exploded almost 1,000 years ago. In its centre is a neutron star. The star spins 30 times a second. The first spinning neutron star, called a pulsar, was discovered in 1967, when British astronomer Jocelyn Bell Burnell recorded radio waves from the star as it turned.

Black hole

A black hole is produced as a star core collapses in on itself. Its gravity is so strong that anything falling onto it is trapped for ever. Even light cannot escape from it and so the hole will appear black.

Islands in the Universe

There are billions of galaxies in the Universe. Each one is a vast group of stars held together by its own gravity. A single galaxy contains billions or trillions of stars and clouds of gas and dust. Galaxies are incredibly large and exist at huge distances apart, like remote islands scattered through space. As we look out from our Galaxy, the Milky Way (right), we can see a few galaxies using our eyes alone – these appear as smudges of light. Powerful telescopes are used to reveal other galaxies and their details.

Breakthrough
In the 1920s, American astronomer Edwin Hubble showed that there are other galaxies besides our own, that they conform to a set of basic shapes, and that galaxies are moving apart.

Galaxy types

Galaxies are grouped according to their shape. A spiral is disc-shaped with a bright central bulge and spiralling arms of stars. In a barred spiral, the centre is bar-shaped with arms at each end of the bar. Ellipticals are ball-shaped, like a football, rugby ball, squashed ball or anywhere in between. The fourth type, the irregular galaxy, has no obvious shape. No two of these are alike.

Shapes
The size of the central bulge and tightness of the arms around the centre in spirals and barred spirals differ from galaxy to galaxy. Above left is spiral NGC 1232 and above right is barred spiral NGC 1300. Elliptical galaxy M32 is lower left and the irregular-shaped Large Magellanic Cloud is lower right.

Milky Way

From inside the Milky Way we can look towards the Galaxy's centre. The concentration of stars makes a milky path of light across the night sky. Dark dust clouds hide more distant stars.

Home Galaxy

The Sun is one of the 500,000 million or so stars that make up the Milky Way Galaxy. Astronomers believe it is a barred spiral, but it is difficult to see its overall shape from our position inside the Galaxy. The Milky Way measures 100,000 light years from side to side (one light year is the distance light travels in a year – 9.46 million million km). Even the smallest galaxy is a few thousand light years across and the biggest is over a million light years wide.

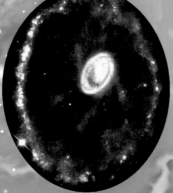

Cartwheel Galaxy

Astronomers use numbers and location co-ordinates to identify galaxies. Some, however, are given unofficial names which cross into regular use. The unusual galaxy above is the Cartwheel – the result of two galaxies colliding.

Clusters

Galaxies exist in clusters, not randomly spread through space. One cluster can contain tens, hundreds or thousands of galaxies. The Coma cluster (above) has at least 1,000 bright galaxies. The Milky Way belongs to a cluster called the Local Group. This includes the Andromeda Galaxy and the Small and Large Magellanic Clouds.

Life

Astronomers are often asked, "Is there life in space?" It is a question no-one can answer with certainty. The Universe is enormous and it would be surprising if Earth were the only place where life existed. But, for the time being at least, it is the only spot where we know for sure that life exists. No life form has been in touch with us on Earth and we have not found any evidence of any living things, past or present, outside of Earth. Astronomers, however, are actively searching for life in space.

Life on Earth

Studying life on Earth helps in the search for life in space. The elements needed for life as we know it – carbon, hydrogen and oxygen – have been found throughout the Universe. We also know that life can survive extreme conditions. Deep in Earth's oceans, hot, chemical-rich water rushes up from volcanic regions, producing smokers (left). Bacteria, a simple, single-celled life form, thrive on the sulphur compounds inside these smokers, without oxygen, and in boiling water.

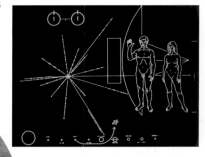

Messages from Earth

Spaceprobes launched from Earth carry messages in case they are found by intelligent life. *Pioneers 10* and *11*, launched in 1972 and 1973, carried a plaque with a plan of the Solar System and human figures. *Voyagers 1* and *2*, launched in 1977, each carried a disc with sounds of Earth.

Searching the Solar System

The planet Mars and Jupiter's moon Europa may be, or have been in the past, home to primitive life forms. Mars is cold now and any water it has is frozen. It was hotter there in the past, and water once flowed across its surface. Primitive life may have developed at that time. Two *Viking* probes landed on Mars in 1976 and tested the soil for signs of life. The results were inconclusive, but the search continues as new probes and robotic vehicles journey to Mars to make further investigations.

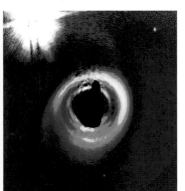

Extra-solar planets
It is likely that life exists on planets outside the Solar System. Astronomers have known of young stars with dust rings, which are forming planets (left), since 1984. The first extra-solar planet was found in 1995. Over 100 more are now known.

Life on Mars?
In 1996, a group of scientists mistakenly thought the microscopic, tube-like structures they were studying in a Martian rock were fossils of a primitive life form.

Outside the Solar System
Astronomers have been searching for intelligent life outside the Solar System for over 40 years. They use radio telescopes, such as the one at Parkes, Australia (right), to listen for signals that may have been sent to us deliberately or transmitted by chance. They are listening in to about 1,000 Sun-like stars, some of which we know have planets.

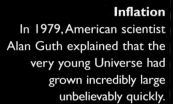

Small Bang
The Big Bang was really quite a small explosion. But almost immediately after it, the Universe inflated. In a tiny fraction of a second it grew from smaller than an atom to bigger than a galaxy.

Beginning to end

The Universe was created in an explosion that astronomers call the Big Bang, about 13 billion years ago. All the material in the Universe today, as well as space and time, was created in that explosion. At first, the material was tiny particles, and these eventually produced today's stars and galaxies. The story of the Universe, from Big Bang to the present, has been pieced together over the last 70 years or so. With each new observation or discovery, astronomers learn more about our past and present, and understand what the future might bring.

First elements
The very young Universe, made of incredibly tiny particles, was unimaginably hot and dense. Within three minutes of the Big Bang, the temperature had dropped to 1 billion °C and the first elements had formed. The Universe was made of about 77 per cent hydrogen and 23 per cent helium, with a minute amount of lithium.

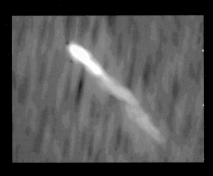

Quasar
When astronomers look into the Universe they look back in time. Objects are so distant it takes their light millions or billions of years to reach us. Quasars (left) are the powerful cores of very remote galaxies. The first was identified by Dutch astronomer Maarten Schmidt in 1963.

First stars and galaxies
The Universe cooled and became less dense as it grew, and about 300,000 years after the Big Bang it became transparent. About 300 million years later, the hydrogen and helium started to form into threads, then clouds, surrounded by empty space. By the time the Universe was about a billion years old these clouds were producing the first stars and galaxies.

Changing Universe
The Universe continues to change. Even now, stars are forming and galaxies are colliding and reshaping, and the whole Universe is still cooling and expanding. Most astronomers believe that it will carry on in this way until, in trillions of years' time, all the stars will have died and the Universe will be a cold, dark place.

Glossary

amateur Someone who does something as a hobby. An amateur astronomer is someone who studies the stars and planets in their leisure time.

asteroid A small rock body orbiting the Sun. Over 90 per cent are in the Main Belt between the orbits of Mars and Jupiter.

astronaut A man or woman who travels into space.

astronomer A person who studies the stars and planets and other objects in space.

astronomy The study of everything in space. That is everything in the Solar System, the Milky Way and everything outside the Milky Way.

atmosphere The layer of gases held around a planet or a moon by its gravity. A star's atmosphere is its layers of gas beyond its photosphere.

atom A tiny particle. An atom is the smallest particle of an element.

aurora A colourful display of light in the sky above Earth's polar regions.

billion One thousand million.

Big Bang The explosion that created the Universe and space and time, about 13,000 million years ago.

black hole The remains of a star that has collapsed in on itself. Its gravity is so strong nothing can get away from it.

brightness A measure of the light of a star. Astronomers measure brightness in two main ways. A scale of apparent brightness gives the brightness of a star seen from Earth. A scale of absolute brightness measures the real brightness of a star.

comet A small snow and dust body. Trillions of comets orbit the Sun beyond the planets. Together they form the Oort Cloud.

constellation A piece of sky whose bright stars form an imaginary pattern, such as that of a human or an animal.

cosmologist Someone who studies the origin, evolution and future of the Universe.

crater A bowl-shaped hollow on the surface of a planet or moon, produced by a meteorite crashing into it.

dark matter The material in the Universe that is invisible to us and has not been found yet. It makes up about 95 per cent of the Universe.

eclipse An effect achieved when one object in space is in the shadow of another. When the Earth's shadow falls on the Moon it is a lunar eclipse. When the Moon covers the Sun and its shadow falls on Earth it is a solar eclipse.

electromagnetic spectrum The range of energy waves that are given off by objects and that travel through space. The waves include light, radio waves, X-rays and infra-red.

element A basic substance of nature such as hydrogen and oxygen.

ellipse A two-dimensional shape. An ellipse is an elongated circle.

equator An imaginary line drawn around the middle of a planet or moon. It divides the top, northern half of the planet or moon from the bottom, southern half.

fossil The remains of something that lived in the past, such as a plant or animal, which is preserved in a planet's surface material.

galaxy A vast number of stars, gas and dust held together by gravity.

gravity A force of attraction found throughout the Universe. The Sun's gravity pulls on Earth, and Earth's pulls on the Moon.

hemisphere One half of a planet or moon. The northern hemisphere is the half above the equator; the southern hemisphere is below.

Kuiper Belt The flat belt of icy rock objects that starts beyond the orbit of Neptune and reaches to the inner edge of the Oort Cloud.

latitude A measure of distance to the north or south of the Earth's equator. Latitude measurement is also used on other planets, moons and the Sun.

light year A measuring unit used by astronomers for distances outside the Solar System. One light year is the distance light travels in one year. That is 9.46 million million km.

luminosity The amount of light produced by a star.

mass The amount of material of which something is made.

meteor The streak of light produced by a meteoroid as it travels through Earth's atmosphere.

meteorite A spacerock that lands on Earth, or on another planet or a moon.

meteoroid A tiny piece of dust from a comet or asteroid, which is no bigger than a grain of sand.

Milky Way The Galaxy we live in. It is also the name of the path of stars in Earth's sky which is our view into the Galaxy's disc.

moon A rock, or rock and icy body that orbits around a planet or an asteroid.

nebula A cloud of gas and dust in space. *See also* planetary nebula.

nuclear fusion The process by which elements inside a star produce other elements. For example, hydrogen atoms fuse to produce helium.

observatory A building or group of buildings which house telescopes used for the observation of the stars and planets.

Oort Cloud The vast sphere of comets that surrounds the Sun and planets.

orbit The path one object takes around another, more massive, object. The Moon follows an orbit around Earth, and Earth orbits the Sun.

photosphere The outer, visible layer of the Sun, or any other star.

planet A large, spherical body made of rock or gas that orbits the Sun or another star.

planetary nebula A type of star that consists of an expanding and colourful cloud of gas and dust, which has been ejected from a dying star.

professional Someone who does something as their job. A professional astronomer is someone who is paid to study the stars and the planets.

pulsar A neutron star (a dense, collapsed star) which spins and sends pulses of energy into space.

quadrant A quarter of a circle. This is also the name for an astronomical instrument, used mainly before the invention of the telescope, to measure the positions of the stars and planets in the sky.

quasar A very bright core of a distant

galaxy. The name is a short form of quasi-stellar object.

radar A technique where radio waves are sent to an object and reflected back to measure the distance of the object. Astronomers use radar to map the surfaces of rocky bodies, such as Venus.

reflector A telescope that uses mirrors to collect and focus light to form an image of a distant object.

refractor A telescope that uses lenses to collect and focus light to form an image of a distant object.

ring system A collection of rings surrounding a planet.

satellite An object held in orbit around a planet or moon by gravity. A telescope in orbit around Earth is a man-made satellite. The Moon is a natural satellite of Earth.

Solar System The Sun and all the objects that orbit around it. These include the nine planets, over 100 moons, billions of spacerocks and trillions of comets.

spaceprobe A type of spacecraft, also called a probe. A spaceprobe is an unmanned craft sent to investigate Solar System objects.

spectrum A spectrum of light is the rainbow band of colours produced when light is split. The plural of spectrum is spectra.

star A sphere of very hot and very luminous gas that produces energy by nuclear fusion.

supernova An old, massive star that has suddenly blown up.

telescope An instrument that uses lenses, mirrors or a combination of the two, to collect light from a distant object and form that light into an image. As well as light, telescopes can also collect other energy, such as radio or X-ray.

trillion One million million.

Universe Everything that exists – all of space and everything in it.

wavelength The distance between the peaks or troughs in waves of electromagnetic radiation.

zodiac The band of 12 constellations that forms the backdrop to the path of the Sun, Moon and planets as they move across the sky.

Index

A

Algol 48, 49
ancient Greeks 9, 48
Andromeda Galaxy 23, 47, 55
Anglo-Australian Observatory 19
Anglo-Australian telescope 15
Antoniadi, Eugène 32
Arecibo radio telescope 18, 19
Ariane rocket 22
Ariel 41
asteroids 25, 36–37, 60
astronauts 22, 31, 60
astronomers 4, 8–9, 10, 11, 12, 13, 14–15, 60
astrophotographers 15
atmosphere 26, 27, 29, 34, 35, 39, 43, 60
aurora 27, 60
Aztecs 9, 44

B

Babylonians 9, 48
BepiColombo probe 32
Betelgeuse 51
Big Bang 15, 58, 60
black holes 53, 60
Brahe, Tycho 10, 11
brown dwarfs 50
Burnell, Jocelyn Bell 53
Butterfly Nebula 52

C

Calar Alto Observatory 17, 18
calendars 9
Canis Major 49
Cannon, Annie Jump 14
Caracol Temple, Mexico 9
Cartwheel Galaxy 55
  Cassini, Giovanni 43
    Cassini probe 23, 43
      Cat's Eye Nebula 53
  Centaurus 49
Ceres 36
Charon 33, 43

Chicxulub Crater 37
chromosphere 26
clusters 13, 55
Coma cluster 55
Comet Hale-Bopp 45
Comet Tempel-Tuttle 45
comets 8, 25, 44–45, 60
constellations 6, 7, 48–49, 60
Copernicus, Nicolaus 10
corona 26, 60
cosmologists 15, 60
Crab Nebula 20, 53
craters 30, 32, 37, 60
Crux 49

D

Dactyl 36
dark matter 21, 60
Deimos 42
Dione 42, 43
Draco 49
dwarf stars 50–51

E

Eagle Nebula 50
Earth 5, 24, 28–9, 56
earthquakes 28
eclipses 8, 26, 60
Eddington, Arthur 46
Egyptian Universe 8
Einstein, Albert 46
electromagnetic spectrum 21, 60
Eratosthenes 9
Eros 36
erosion 28
Eta Carinae 53
Europa 43, 57
European Southern Observatory 18, 19
exploding stars 53
extra-solar planets 57

F

flares 26

G

galaxies 5, 11, 47, 54–55, 59, 60
Galileo Galilei 12, 13, 40
Galileo probe 38, 39
Galle, Johann 41
gamma rays 21
Ganymede 42
gas planets 25, 38–41
Gaspra 36
Gemini 48
giant stars 50–51
Giotto spaceprobe 44
Glaisher, James 29
gravity 5, 21, 24, 27, 60
Great Dark Spot 41
Great Red Spot 38
Guth, Alan 58

H

Halley, Edmond 44
Halley's Comet 44
Harvard College Observatory 14
helium 27, 38, 58
Hercules 49
Herschel, William 13, 41
Hertzsprung, Ejnar 50
Hoyle, Fred 15
Hubble, Edwin 54
Hubble Space Telescope 14, 33, 41
Huygens, Christiaan 40
Huygens probe 23
hydrogen 27, 38, 40, 58

I

Iapetus 43
Ida 36
infra-red waves 20, 21
Io 43

J

Jansky, Karl 21
Janus 42
Jupiter 23, 25, 38–39, 40, 42, 43

K
Keck telescopes 16, 17
Kepler, Johannes 10, 11
Kitt Peak National Observatory 18, 19
Kuiper Belt 25, 33, 36, 60

L
Large Magellanic Cloud 54, 55
Leonid meteor shower 45
Lick Observatory 19
life 28, 43, 56–57
light waves 20, 21
Local Group galaxy cluster 55
Lockyer, Norman 27
Lowell Observatory 33, 35
Lowell, Percival 35
luminosity 47, 60

M
Maat Mons 34
Magellan probe 34
Main Belt 36
Main Sequence stars 50
Malin, David 15
maria 31
Mariner 10 probe 32
Mars 5, 22, 24, 25, 34, 35, 37, 42, 57
Mauna Kea Observatories 16, 17, 18
Mayan people 9
measuring 9, 11
Mercury 24, 25, 32, 42
Messenger probe 32
meteorites 37, 60
meteoroids 37, 61
meteors 45, 60
Milky Way Galaxy 6, 8, 11, 21, 55, 61
Miranda 41
Moon 5, 7, 13, 22, 30–31, 37
moons 23, 25, 33, 36, 39, 41, 42–43, 61

N
NEAR probe 36
nebulae 6, 15, 20, 50, 53, 61
Neptune 25, 33, 40, 41, 43
neutron stars 53
Newton, Isaac 13

O
Oberon 41
observatories 4, 9, 13, 17, 18–19, 61
Olympus Mons 35
Oort Cloud 25, 44, 61
orbits 11, 24, 32, 33, 36, 61
Orion 6, 48, 51
Orion Nebula 6, 15

P
Parkes Observatory 19, 57
Pathfinder 22
Perseus 48, 49
phases of the Moon 30
Phobos 42
Phoenix 49
photosphere 26, 61
Pioneer spaceprobes 38, 56
planetary nebulae 52–53, 61
planets 5, 7, 11, 24–25, 38–41, 57, 61
Pluto 24, 25, 32, 33, 43
prisms 13
Ptolemy, Claudius 10
pulsars 53, 61

Q
quasars 59, 61

R
radio telescopes 18, 19, 20, 57
radio waves 20, 21
Red Spider Nebula 52
red supergiants 6, 51
reflectors 13, 17, 61
refractors 13, 61
Rhea 43
ringed planets 40–41
rock planets 25, 32–35
rockets 22
Rosetta probe 44
Royal Observatory, Greenwich 18
Russell, Henry 50

S
satellites 22, 28, 61
Saturn 23, 25, 40–41, 42, 43
Schmidt, Maarten 59
Scorpius 49

shooting stars 45
Sirius 49
Small Magellanic Cloud 55
Sojourner 22
Solar System 24–25, 36, 61
space telescopes 14, 23, 33, 41
spacecraft 14, 22–23, 44
spaceprobes 22, 23, 32, 34, 39, 44, 56, 61
spacerocks 25, 36–37
spectrum 13, 61
Spirograph Nebula 52
Stardust probe 44
stars 6, 7, 11, 14, 46, 47, 48–49, 50–51, 52–53, 54–55, 59
Subaru telescope 16
Sun 6, 24, 26–27, 51
sunspots 26
supernovae 47, 53, 61

T
Taurus 48
telescopes 4, 12, 13, 15, 16–17, 23
Tethys 42, 43
Titan 23, 43
Titania 41
Triton 43
Tombaugh, Clyde 33

U
ultraviolet waves 21
Umbriel 41
Universe 4–5, 8, 10–11, 58–59, 61
Uranus 13, 25, 40, 41, 43

V
Valles Marineris 35
Vela supernova 47
Venus 9, 24, 25, 34, 42
Very Large Array 21
Very Large Telescope (VLT) 17
Viking probes 57
volcanoes 28, 34, 35
Voyager probes 38, 40, 41, 42, 56

W
water 24, 28, 29
wavelengths 20, 21, 61
Whipple, Fred 44
white dwarfs 51
WIMPs (weakly interactive massive particles) 21
Wolfe Creek Crater 37

XYZ
X-rays 20, 21, 23
XMM-Newton space telescope 23
zodiac 7, 61

Acknowledgements

The publisher would like to thank the following for permission to reproduce their material. Every care has been taken to trace copyright holders. However, if there have been unintentional omissions or failure to trace copyright holders, we apologise and will, if informed, endeavour to make corrections in any future edition.

The publisher would like to thank the following illustrators for their contributions to this book:
b = bottom, *c* = centre, *l* = left, *r* = right, *t* = top
Jonathan Adams 13 *br*; **Julian Baker** 36; **Julian Baum** 23 *tr*, 27 *tr*, 31 *tr*, 33 *b*, 44–45, 49 *r*, 53 *bl*; **Mark Bristow** 24–25, 38–39; **Terry Gabbey (AFA O Ltd)** 9 *t*; **Alan Hancocks** 22–23 *b*, 34–35, 40–41, 50–51 *br*, 58–59; **Mike Roffe** 23 *tc*; **Mike White** 8–9 *b*; **Gareth Williams** 16–17, 48–49.

The publisher would like to thank the following for supplying photographs for this book:
b = bottom, *c* = centre, *l* = left, *t* = top
Pages: cover Corbis/© Roger Ressmeyer; **4** *bl* SPL (Science Photo Library)/Magrath Photography; **4** *br* SPL/Frank Zullo; **5** *cl* Galaxy Picture Library/JPL; **5** *tr* SPL/Canada-France-Hawaii Telescope/Jean-Charles Cuillandre; **5** *tc* SPL/Dr Jean Lorre; **5** *cr* SPL/David Nunuk; **5** *br* SPL/Simon Fraser; **6-7** SPL/Dennis Milon/Allan Morton; **6** *bl* SPL/John Chumack; **7** *tl* David Malin Images/David Miller; **8** *tr* Werner Forman Archive/Private Collection; **9** *tl* Corbis/Danny Lehman; **10** *tl* SPL/Detlev van Ravenswaay; **10** *c* SPL/J-L. Charmet; **10** *cr* Bridgeman Art Library/British Library, London, UK; **11** *tl* SPL; **11** *tr* SPL/NASA/Space Telescope Science Institute; **11** *br* Corbis/Bettman; **12** *bl* AKG Images; **12** *bc* Science and Society Picture Library/Science Museum; **13** *tr* SPL/David Parker; **13** *c* Science and Society Picture Library/Science Museum; **14** *tr* Corbis/Hulton-Deutsch Collection; **14** *b* SPL/David Parker; **15** *tl* Corbis/Hulton-Deutsch Collection; **15** *bc* Anglo-Australian Observatory/David Malin; **15** *br* Corbis/© Roger Ressmeyer; **16** *cr* Corbis/© Roger Ressmeyer; **17** *tr* European Southern Observatory/Pierre Kervella; **17** *bl* Bruce Coleman Collection/Astrofoto; **18** *bl* Royal Astronomical Society; **19** *tr* Corbis/Roger Ressmeyer; **19** *c* Corbis/Stephanie Maze; **19** *cr* Bruce Coleman Collection/European Southern Observatory; **19** *br* SPL/David Nunuk; **20** *bl* Corbis/© Roger Ressmeyer; **20** *tr* NASA/CXC/SAO; **21** *tr* SPL/IAP/Yannick Mellier; **22** *tr* SPL/NASA; **22** *bl* SPL/European Space Agency; **23** *cl* European Space Agency; **24** Science and Society Picture Library/Science Museum; **25** © National Maritime Museum, London; **26** *b* Trace Project/NASA; **26** *tr* Science and Society Picture Library/NASA; **27** *bl* SPL/Chris Madeley; **27** *cr* Science and Society Picture Library/Science Museum; **28** *tr* SPL/European Space Agency; **28** *bl* SPL/Dr Morley Read; **28** *bcl* Still Pictures/© Otto Hahn; **28** *bcr* Corbis/David Muench; **28** *br* SPL/Bernhard Edmaier; **29** *tl* Science and Society Picture Library/Science Museum; **29** *br* Corbis/© 1996, original image courtesy of NASA; **30** *tr* SPL/David Nunuk; **31** *br* SPL/NASA; **32** *tl* Royal Astronomical Society; **33** *tl* Corbis/© Bettman; **34** *bl* NASA/NSSDC; **35** *tr* Corbis/Bettman; **36** *tr* SPL/NASA; **36** *br* Galaxy Picture Library/JPL; **36** *bl* Galaxy Picture Library/JPL; **37** *tl* Galaxy Picture Library/Howard Miles; **37** *cr* SPL/Worldsat International Inc; **37** *c* SPL/Michael Abbey; **37** *br* Antarctic Search for Meteorites Program/W. A. Cassidy; **38** *cl* Galaxy Picture Library/JPL; **39** *tr* Art Archive/Palazzo del Te Mantua/Dagli Orti (A); **39** *cr* Galaxy Picture Library/Robin Scagell; **39** *br* NASA/JPL/California Institute of Technology; **40** *bl* Galaxy Picture Library/JPL; **40** *cr* SPL; **41** *cl* Galaxy Picture Library/STScI; **41** *bl* SPL/NASA; **41** *cr* Galaxy Picture Library/JPL; **41** *br* European Southern Observatory; **42** *tr* SPL/NASA; **42** *bl* Galaxy Picture Library/JPL; **42** *br* Galaxy Picture Library/Calvin J. Hamilton; **43** *tl* SPL; **43** *cl* Galaxy Picture Library/OPM/Athéne Coustenis; **43** *bl* SPL/NASA; **43** *br* Galaxy Picture Library/JPL; **44** *tr* SPL/European Space Agency; **44** *bl* Bridgeman Art Library/Bridgeman Art Library Giraudon/Biblioteca Nacional, Madrid, Spain; **45** *tr* SPL/John Chumack; **45** *bc* SPL/David Mclean; **46** *tr* © Institute of Astronomy, University of Cambridge; **46** *bl* SPL/National Optical Astronomy Observatories (NOAO); **47** *tr* Robert Gendler; **47** *br* SPL/Celestial Image Co; **48** © Bodleian Library, Oxford; **50** *bl* SPL/NASA/Space Telescope Science Institute; **50** *tc* es.geocities.com; **50** *tr* Lorand Eöyvös University Gothard Astrophysical Observatory; **51** *t* SPL/Lynette Cook; **51** *cl* NASA/A Dupree (CfA) & R Cilliland (STScI); **52** *tr* NASA/JPL/R Sahai; **52** *tl* NASA/ESA/HST/Garrelt Mellema (Leiden University); **52** *bc* SPL/NASA/Space Telescope Science Institute; **53** *tl* SPL/NASA/Space Telescope Science Institute; **53** *tr* NOAO/AURA/NSF; **53** *bc* SPL/Robin Scagell; **53** *br* NASA; **54** *tl* SPL; **54** *cl* European Southern Observatory (ESO); **54** *c* NSF/AURA/NOAO/Hilary Mathis; **54** *bl* NASA; **54** *br* NASA; **55** *tr* SPL/Dr Fred Espenak; **55** *bc* Galaxy Picture Library/STScI; **55** *br* SPL/Celestial Image Co; **56** *l* Galaxy Picture Library/NOAO/NURP/OAR; **56** *bc* Galaxy Picture Library/JPL; **56** *br* SPL/NASA; **57** *tr* Galaxy Picture Library/NASA; **57** *c* NASA/M Clampin (STScI), H Ford (JHU), G Illingworth (UCO/Lick), J Krist (STScI), D Ardila (JHU), D Golimowski (JHU), the ACS Science Team and ESA; **57** *br* SPL/Dr Seth Shostak; **58** *tr* SPL/David Parker; **59** *tl* Galaxy Picture Library/Cavendish Laboratory; **59** *tr* Galaxy Picture Library/NASA/Space Telescope Science Institute; **Endpapers** Royal Astronomical Society.

Below is a list of useful websites:
www.ras.org.uk (The Royal Astronomical Society)
www.nmm.ac.uk (The Royal Observatory, Greenwich)
www.nasa.gov (NASA)
www.esa.int/export/esaCP/index.html (European Space Agency Portal)